The DINOSAUR Colouring Book

Buster Books

Illustrated by
Jake McDonald

Edited by Hannah Cohen
Designed by Zoe Bradley
Cover designed by
John Bigwood

First published in Great Britain in 2015
by Buster Books, an imprint of
Michael O'Mara Books Limited, 9 Lion Yard,
Tremadoc Road, London SW4 7NQ

www.busterbooks.co.uk

Buster Children's Books

@BusterBooks

ISBN: 978-1-78055-351-1

4 6 8 10 9 7 5 3

This book was printed in January 2017 by
Shenzhen Wing King Tong Paper Products
Co. Ltd., Shenzhen, Guangdong, China.

These dinosaurs were coloured
and completed by

....

TOP TIP: Scientists don't know what colour
the dinosaurs really were, so go wild and
colour them in any colours you like.

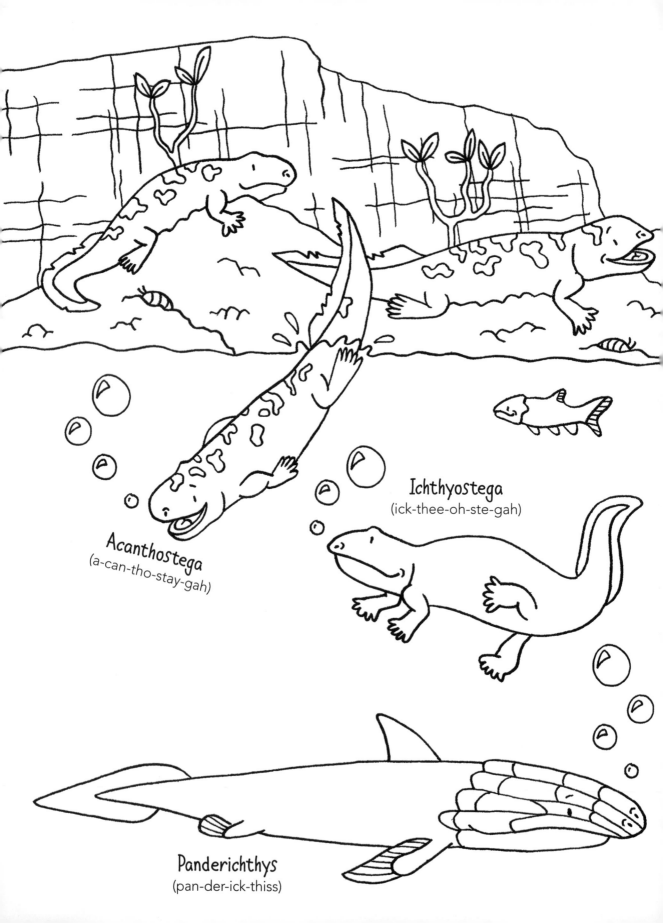

Acanthostega
(a-can-tho-stay-gah)

Ichthyostega
(ick-thee-oh-ste-gah)

Panderichthys
(pan-der-ick-thiss)

400 million years ago, fish began to grow legs and walk on to the land.

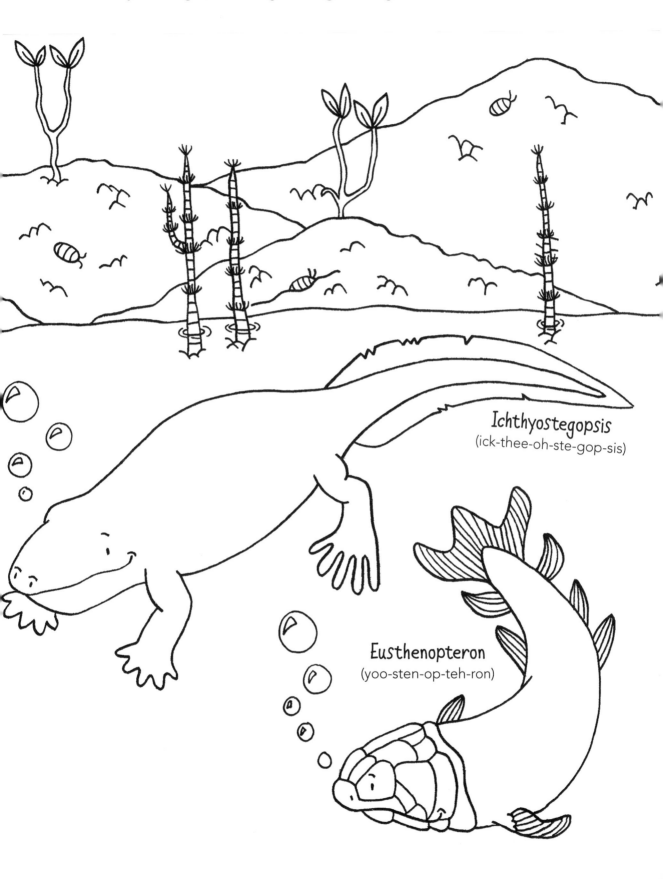

Ichthyostegopsis
(ick-thee-oh-ste-gop-sis)

Eusthenopteron
(yoo-sten-op-teh-ron)

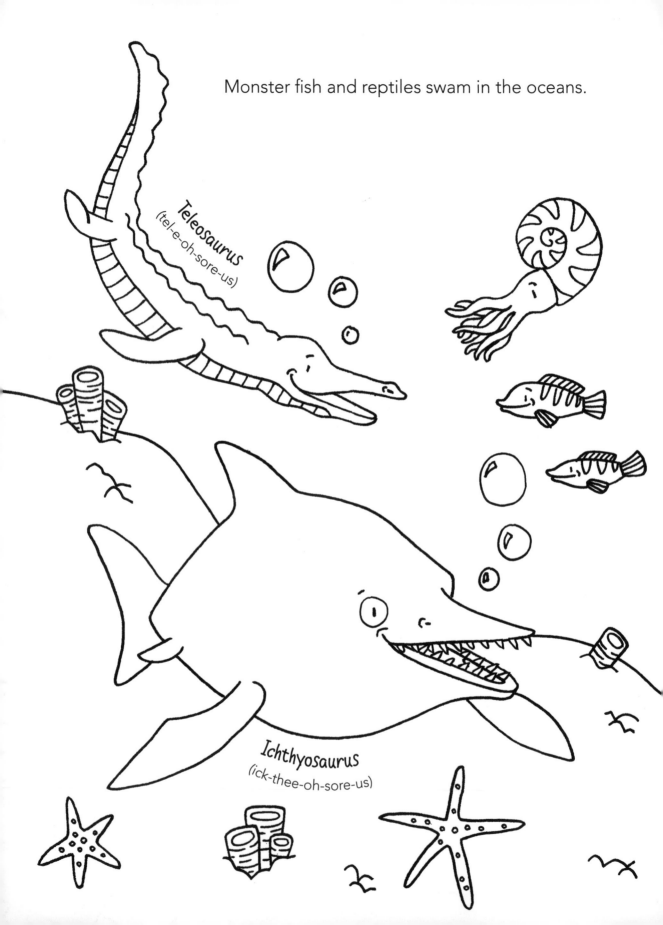

Monster fish and reptiles swam in the oceans.

Teleosaurus
(tel-e-oh-sore-us)

Ichthyosaurus
(ick-thee-oh-sore-us)

Eurhinosaurus
(yoo-rye-no-sore-us)

King crab

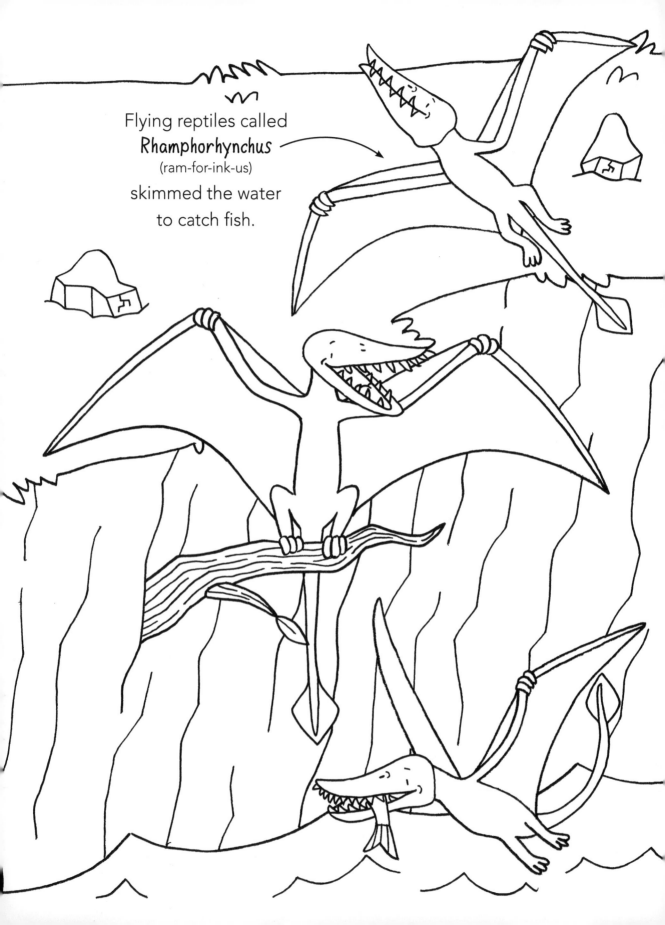

Flying reptiles called
Rhamphorhynchus
(ram-for-ink-us)
skimmed the water
to catch fish.

Kentrosaurus
(ken-troh-sore-us)

The biggest dinosaurs lived 150 million years ago.

Diplodocus
(di-plod-oh-kus)

Pterodactylus
(teh-roh-dack-till-us)

Stegosaurus
(steg-oh-sore-us)

Eosipterus
(ee-oh-sigh-tair-us)

Jinzhousaurus
(jeen-joh-sore-us)

Sinornithosaurus
(sine-or-nith-o-sore-us)

These bird-like dinosaurs were covered in feathers.

Acrocanthosaurus
(ah-kroh-kan-tho-sore-us)
grew up to 11 metres
long and had 68 sharp
teeth to munch its
prey with.

Pterodactylus
(teh-roh-dack-till-us)

Planicoxa
(plan-ee-coks-ah)

Plateosaurus
(plat-ee-oh-sore-us)

Rutiodon (roo-tie-oh-don) had thicker
and heavier armour than that of the
crocodiles that live today.

Liliensternus
(lil-ee-en-shtern-us)

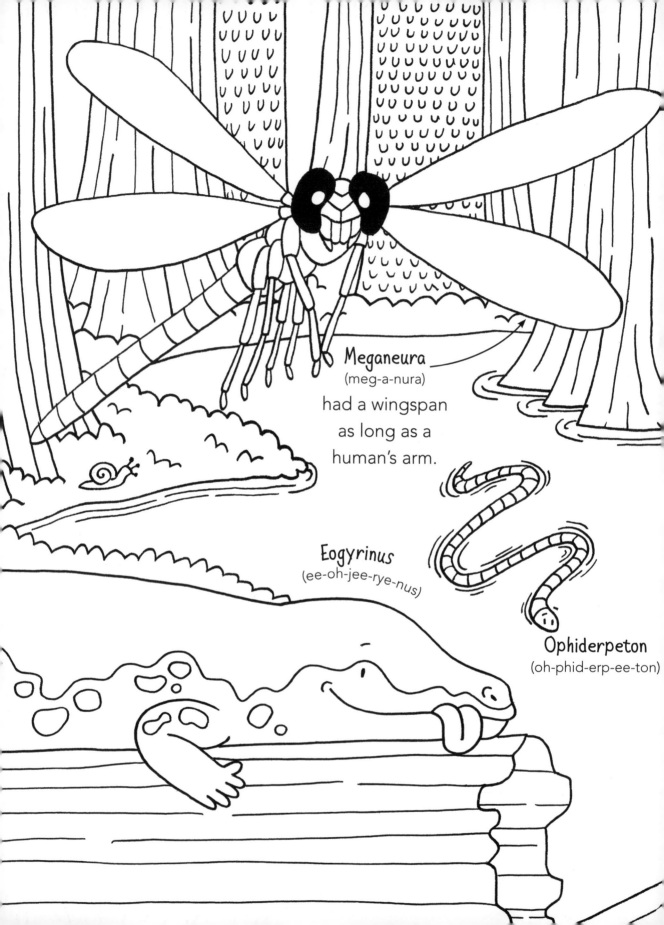

Meganeura
(meg-a-nura)
had a wingspan
as long as a
human's arm.

Eogyrinus
(ee-oh-jee-rye-nus)

Ophiderpeton
(oh-phid-erp-ee-ton)

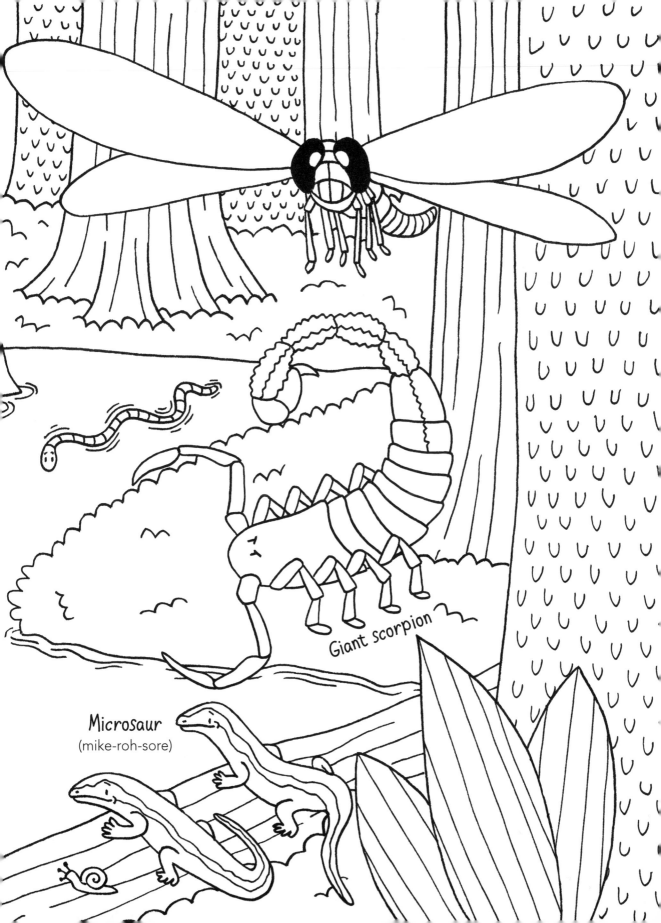

Giant Scorpion

Microsaur
(mike-roh-sore)

Edaphosaurus
(ee-daff-oh-sore-us)
had a sail on its back that may have warmed up its body in the sun.

Cacops
(cay-cops)

Protorosaurus
(pro-tor-oh-sore-us)

Scutosaurus
(scoot-oh-sore-us)

Parasaurolophus
(pa-ra-sore-rol-off-us)
may have used the tube-shaped
crest on its head to make
its calls louder.

Fossilized ammonites

Stagonolepis
(stag-on-oh-lep-is)
had a big snout
to dig up roots
and plants to eat.

Plateosaurus
(plat-ee-oh-sore-us)

Staurikosaurus
(stor-ik-oh-sore-us)
may have hunted
in packs.

Kentrosaurus (ken-troh-sore-us) had a small skull and a little brain.

Tanystropheus (tan-ee-stro-fee-us) used its long neck to catch fish.

Kuehneosaurus (keen-ee-oh-sore-us) had thin wings made of skin that it may have used to glide or parachute from trees.

The bony plates on the back of
Stegosaurus (steg-oh-sore-us)
may have helped it to control
its body temperature.

Desmatosuchus
(dez-mat-oh-soo-kus)
had long spikes on its
shoulders to protect it
from predators.

Coelophysis
(seel-oh-fie-sis)
could run fast.

Megapnosaurus
(me-gap-noh-sore-us)

Maiasaura (my-oh-sore-ah) looked after its young in a nest and brought them leaves to eat.

Thecodontosaurus (theek-oh-don-toh-sore-us) probably ran on four legs but spent most of its time standing on its two back legs.

The mighty
Tyrannosaurus rex
(tie-ran-oh-sore-us rex)
could grow up to
14 metres long.

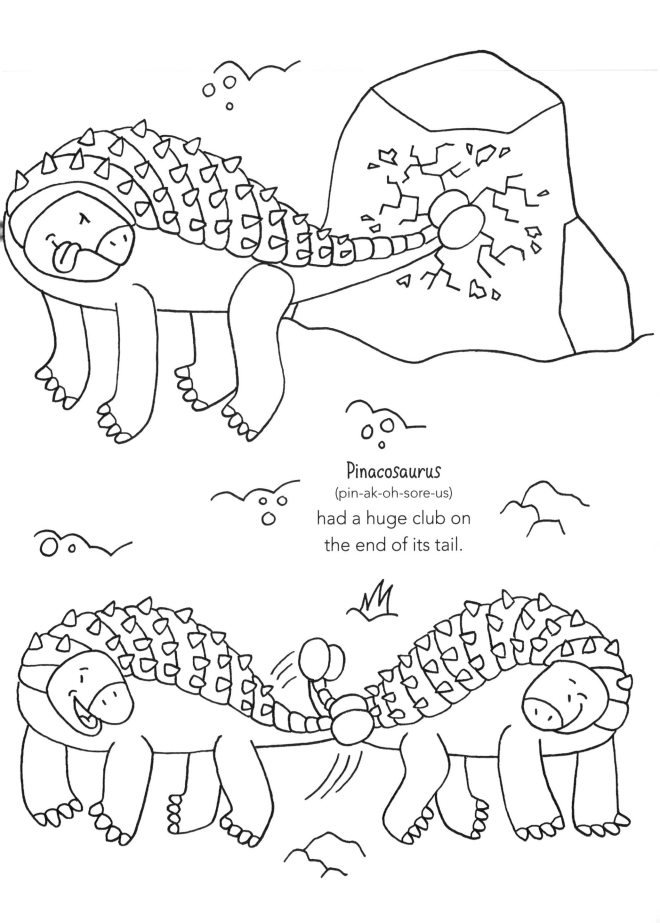

Pinacosaurus
(pin-ak-oh-sore-us)
had a huge club on
the end of its tail.

Protoceratops
(pro-toh-ser-ah-tops)
laid its eggs in a nest
in the sand.

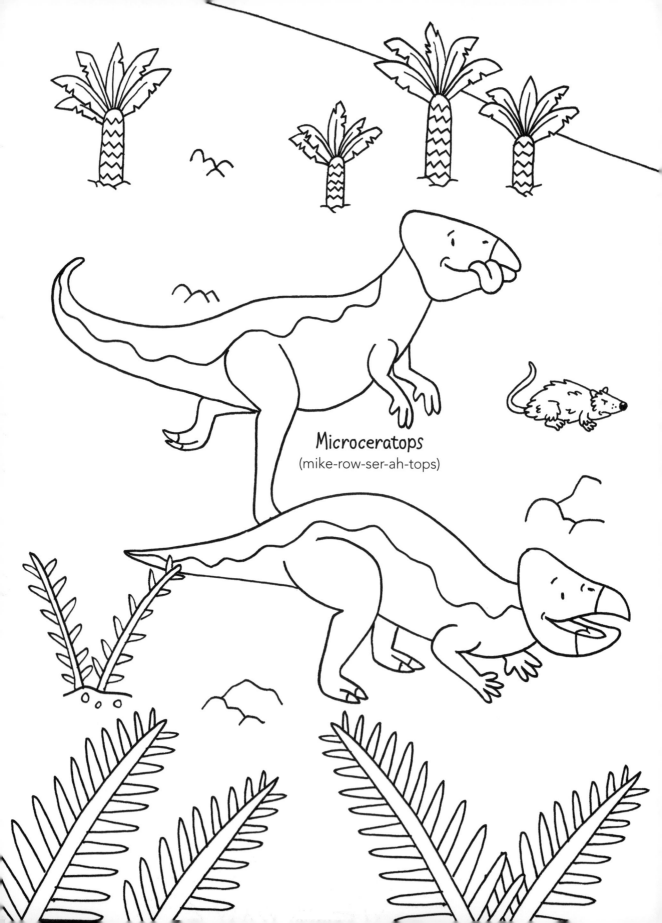

Microceratops
(mike-row-ser-ah-tops)

Velociraptor
(vel-oss-ee-rap-tor)

was a ferocious hunter.

Giganotosaurus
(gig-an-oh-toe-sore-us)
looked a bit like a T. rex,
but it was even bigger.

Tyrannosaurus
(tie-ran-oh-sore-us)

had tiny arms compared
to the size of its body.

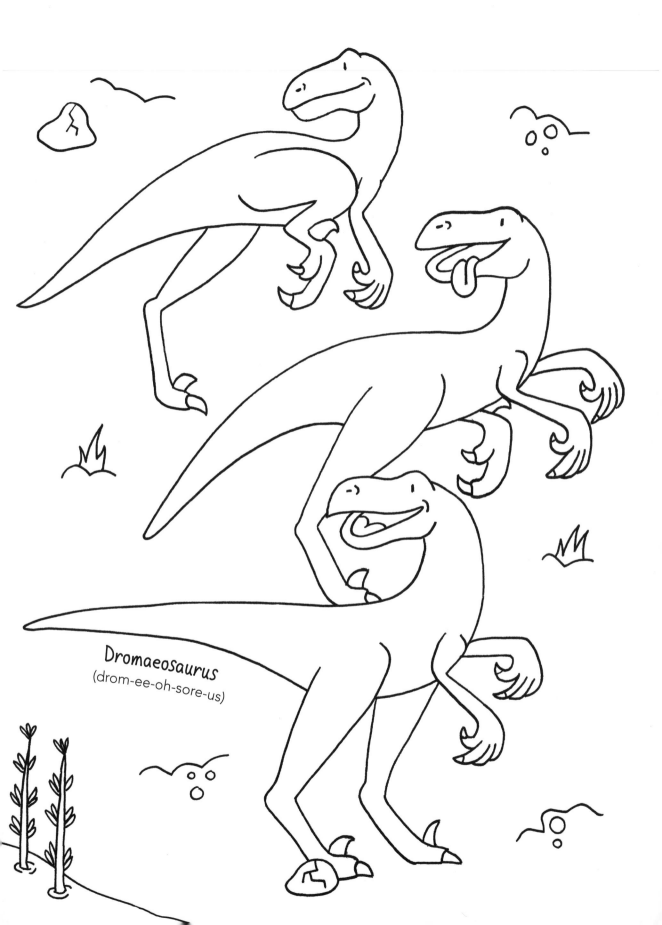

Dromaeosaurus
(drom-ee-oh-sore-us)

The name **Oviraptor**
(oh-vee-rap-tor)
means 'egg thief'
but it isn't known if these
dinosaurs really stole eggs.

The earliest known bird, **Archaeopteryx** (ark-ee-opt-er-icks) had features of both a bird and a dinosaur.

An early reptile called **Hylonomus** (hy-lon-oh-mus) lived in hollow stumps and ate the insects that lived there.

Ankylosaurus
(an-kie-loh-sore-us)
used its tail as a
weapon to fight
its enemies.

Uintatherium
(win-tah-thee-ree-um)

Diatryma
(die-ah-tree-ma)

Even after the dinosaurs died out, giant birds and strange mammals still roamed the earth.

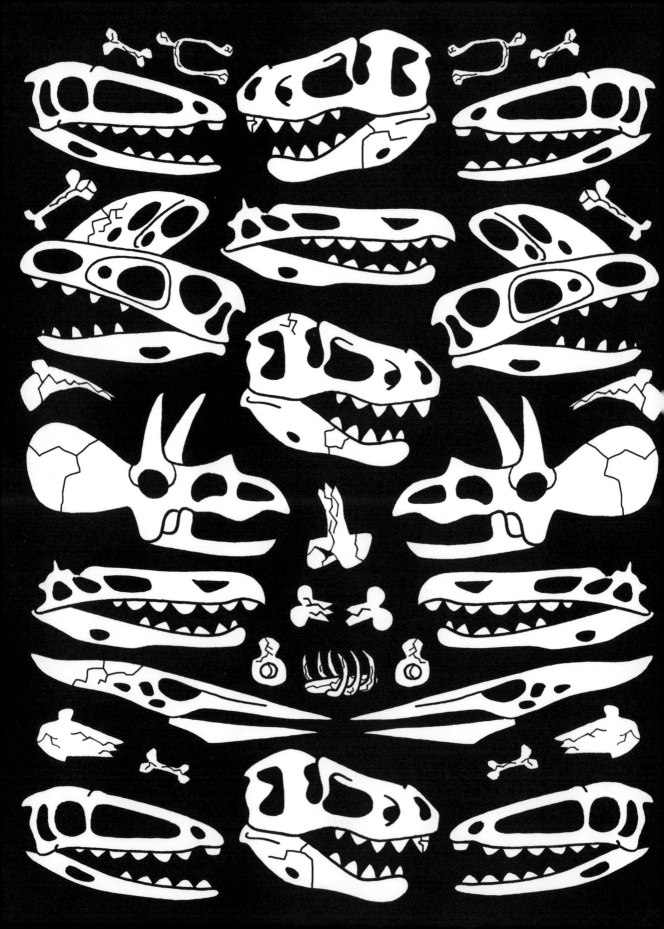

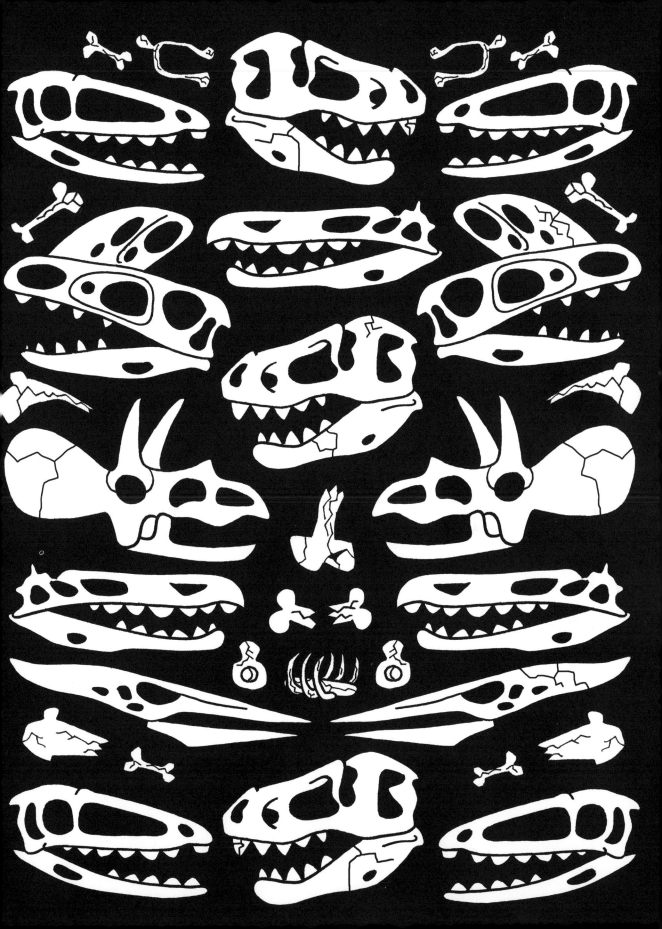

Teratornis
(ter-a-torn-is)

Ground *sloths* had bony
lumps under their
skin to protect them
against predators.

Sabre-toothed cat

Cave lion

Woolly rhino

During the Ice Age, the temperature changed from warm to cold and the mammals grew thick fur on their bodies to keep warm.

Woolly mammoths

Super skeletons